How to Be Kind

Making the World a Better Place through Empathy & Compassion

Written & Illustrated by Kristie Zoller, PsyD

How to Be Kind

Making the World a Better Place through Empathy & Compassion

All marketing and publishing rights guaranteed to and reserved by:

(817) 277-0727

www.fhautism.com

ISBN: 978-1-963367-38-6

Contents

Contents

A Note to Adults Who Care for Children

When I began writing this book, I was in a dark place, fueled by the injustice, violence, and global health issues I was observing in the world ... Normally, I'm an upbeat, optimistic person, but I found myself dwelling on the worst of what I was seeing from people. I know there is more goodness in the world than hate, but it's harder to find. Studies show that we pay more attention to negative information, as it is far more gripping and engaging. But as a psychologist, I've seen how positivity and kindness can benefit our mood and well-being. I knew that I couldn't surrender to hatred and darkness, so instead, I refocused my attention on the goodness in others. To feel better about my world, I needed to help create more kindness, something that can never be in excess. It was in my work that I found my light.

I work in a job where emotions are my specialty. Using genuine kindness, empathy, and respect to connect with children, adolescents, and their families is critical to building therapeutic relationships. Not surprisingly, these attributes are also important building blocks for any relationship, and in my opinion, one can never be too young to start practicing kindness. As adults, we have principles and philosophies that we use to help us understand our world and make effective decisions, but the morals and values of our children are still being molded.

Engaged parents, guardians, and other caregivers, such as teachers and therapists, have the strongest impact on molding the minds and actions of young people. It is our job as adults to help children determine what is right and wrong, teach them how to safely express their emotions, and model respectful behavior toward others. In doing so, we can ensure they grow into loving and positive individuals who appreciate differences in others, defend the defenseless, and fight for what is right, good, and just.

Please use this workbook as a tool to help cultivate kindness in your children. The activities are meant for you and your children to complete together, and they should be used to help start conversations about the topics of kindness, emotions, and self-care. The time you set aside to work on these activities can also be used to create a safe and open environment for other meaningful discussions. You are the role model, and the book is your tool to help you impart these important lessons.

Why Is It Important to Be Kind?

Being kind means that you want to do good for others and show you care about them. You can be kind to people, animals, and the earth. But why is it important to be kind? Being kind makes others feel happy and shows them how much you love and care for them. We're kind to people because they're special and deserve to be treated with respect, we're kind to animals because they're part of our family and rely on us to feed and care for them, and we're kind to insects because they help our planet grow. We're kind to plants and the earth because their nutrients help us all live and be healthy. Being kind makes other people feel good about themselves and makes you feel good about yourself too! Being kind helps all of us blossom.

Draw a picture of you doing something kind.

Introduction to the Be Kind Strategies

In this workbook, you'll learn many ways to be kind. Some might be simple, and others might take a lot of work, but being kind doesn't have to be hard. As you'll learn, even things like smiling or holding the door open for someone can show people that you care about them.

First, you'll learn about yourself. You might wonder why you're learning about yourself in a book about being kind to others. But learning about what you're good at and being kind to yourself will help make it easier for you to be kind to others. When you feel good about yourself, you can help others feel good about themselves too! It's important to be a good role model. A *role model* is someone people look up to. If people see you being kind to yourself, they'll want to be kind too.

Next, you'll learn strategies or ways you can be kind to others. You'll talk to new people, spend time helping others, and learn about other people's lives. Sometimes you might be asked to change how you act with other people in order to be kinder and more thoughtful. Along the way, you might think of some new ways to be kind too. That's because you're such a creative person! **When you think of new ways to be kind, write them down at the end of this book under "My Own Be Kind Strategies" on page 91.**

Introduction

The goal of this workbook is to teach you ways to be kind to yourself and others.

Follow Buttercup the Bee, and you'll see that as you learn to be kind, more flowers will bloom because Buttercup is energized by your kindness and so proud of you! She's so happy to see the world becoming a better place with your kindness, and she's motivated to do her part to make the world even more beautiful too!

Strategy

Take Care of Myself

Before learning about ways to be kind to others, it's important to learn how to be kind to yourself. When you feel happy and strong and believe in yourself, it's called being *confident*. When you're confident, it's easy to share that confidence with others by being kind. What does it mean to take care of yourself? In order to take good care of yourself, you need to do the things that make you feel happy, make you feel good about yourself, and keep you healthy.

For example, Buttercup the Bee feels happy when she's flying around with her friends. When she helps to build a strong hive, she feels good about herself. When she exercises, she feels healthy. **Fill out the lists on the next page to share ways that you can take care of yourself.**

Strategy 1

Things that make me feel happy:

1.

2.

3.

Things that keep me healthy:

1.

2.

3.

Things that make me feel good about myself:

1.

2.

3.

Now that you know what you like to do to take care of yourself, **pick one of the activities you listed and write it below. Circle the words that describe how you felt while doing the activity**. You don't have to keep track of all of your activities, but remembering how good you feel will remind you how important it is to take care of yourself.

Activity: ______________________________

How I felt doing it:

Happy	Creative	Cheerful
Useful	Relaxed	Hopeful
Excited	Strong	Motivated
Proud	Brave	Healthy
Peaceful	Optimistic	Safe
Joyful	Eager	Thankful
Brilliant	Content	Glad
Calm	Playful	Delighted
Athletic	Grateful	Curious
Confident	Surprised	Appreciated

Strategy

Learn about My Emotions

Emotions is another word for *feelings*. *Feelings* are the reactions we have to what is going on around us. We can have lots of different feelings. Learning about how we feel and what we do when we feel a certain way is important because it can help us be in control of our emotions.

The more we learn about our emotions, the better we become at telling others how we feel so we can get help or what we need. Then, we can work to make sure we feel good and other people feel good too.

In the circles on the next page, draw faces to match the emotion.

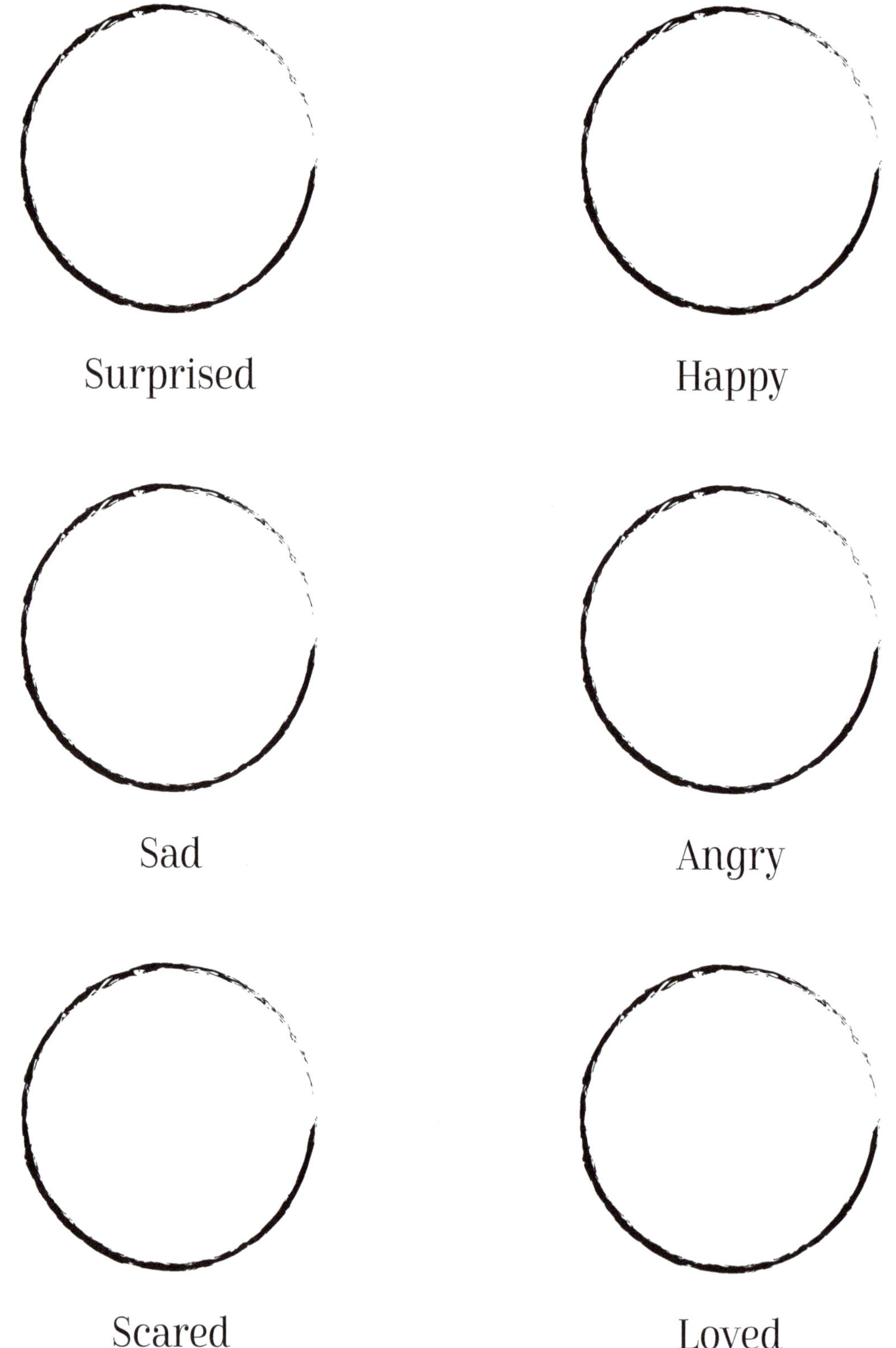
Surprised
Happy
Sad
Angry
Scared
Loved

Strategy 2

You can't always help how you feel, but you can definitely choose how you communicate your emotions. Sometimes you might **communicate** your feelings using words, and other times you might use actions. For example, you might express love by saying, "I love you," which is a way to communicate using words, or by hugging a person, which is a way to communicate using actions. Learning to tell others how you feel using respectful language and actions can help others understand what you're going through and what you need. Sharing your emotions respectfully is a great way to be kind! **With the help of the example provided by Buttercup the Bee, share how you communicate your feelings on the next page.**

Example from Buttercup

1. **What happened and how did you feel?**
   My friend wouldn't let me play with his toy cars, and I felt angry.

2. **How did you communicate your emotions?**
   I took the cars from my friend so I could play with them.

3. **Were you respectful? If not, what could you do differently next time?**
   No, I wasn't respectful. Next time, I could ask my friend nicely to play with his cars. If he says no, then I can ask him if he can share one of his cars when he's finished playing with it.

1. **What happened and how did you feel?**

2. **How did you communicate your emotions?**

3. **Were you respectful? If not, what could you do differently next time?**

Strategy

Remember When Others Were Kind to Me

During your life, there have been many times when people have been kind to you. A teacher might have complimented you on your art project, or a friend might have made a card for you. It's nice to remember when others were kind to you. Looking back on all of these times can lift your spirits when you're feeling down and help you remember how important you are to other people. They can also inspire you to be kind to others.

Using the boxes on the next page, write down and keep track of when people are kind to you.

Remember, kindness can mean doing something simple, like saying, "Thank you," or something more complex, like when someone you love makes cookies to celebrate your good grades.

Example from Buttercup

My friend shared her lunch with me when I forgot mine at home.

Remember to look back on these kindnesses every so often to remind yourself that people have been kind to you because they care about you and think you're special.

Strategy 4

Meditate and Be Mindful

What does it mean to meditate? *Meditating* means to relax and calm yourself in a specific way, often by giving your full attention to only one thing at a time. Meditating helps you become more aware of your body while helping to quiet what is going on around you. If you find your mind wandering away from the activity, that's okay. Just turn the channel in your head back and continue your meditation. There are many ways to meditate, and we'll learn a few now.

Deep Breathing

Deep breathing means to slowly fill your lungs with air so your chest and stomach expand and then breathe out slowly to calm your body. While you are breathing, you should focus on how your body feels. Feel the air flow into your nose, how your lungs fill with air, and how your mouth feels when you release the air. **Have the adult you're working with read the exercise on the next page while you're sitting or reclining in a comfortable place.**

Deep Breathing Exercise

1. Close your eyes and focus on the calm sound of my voice.

2. Now,* take a very deep breath slowly through your nose while you count silently to 5.

3. Place your hands on your lower stomach. Focus on how the air feels flowing in through your nose and how your stomach expands ... 1 ... 2 ... 3 ... 4 ... 5 ...

4. Now, slowly breathe out through your mouth like you are blowing bubbles. Blow gently so you don't pop the bubbles. And count to five while you're blowing out ... 1 ... 2 ... 3 ... 4 ... 5 ...

5. Stay focused on how the air feels flowing out of your mouth. Let's do this exercise five more times.

* Repeat from here five additional times.

Progressive Muscle Relaxation

Progressive muscle relaxation is a way of tensing and loosening one set of muscles at a time so you feel calm. **Have the adult you're working with read the exercise on the next page while you're sitting or reclining in a comfortable position.** Follow along and remember to keep breathing slowly and deeply.

Strategy 4

Progressive Muscle Relaxation Exercise

1. Close your eyes.

2. Slowly, take a deep breath, in through your nose and out through your mouth. One more time, in through your nose and out through your mouth.

3. Now, squeeze your eyes closed tightly. Hold 1 ... 2 ... 3 ... 4 ... 5 ... and relax your eyes.

4. Now, press your lips together tightly. Hold 1 ... 2 ... 3 ... 4 ... 5 ... and relax your lips.

5. Next, lean your head to your left shoulder and feel how your neck tightens on the right side. Hold 1 ... 2 ... 3 ... 4 ... 5 ... and relax your neck.

6. Now, lean your head to your right shoulder and feel how your neck tightens on the left side. Hold 1 ... 2 ... 3 ... 4 ... 5 ... and relax.

7. Next, press your chin down to your chest and feel how the back of your neck feels. Hold 1 ... 2 ... 3 ... 4 ... 5 ... and relax.

8. Now, slowly open your eyes and feel how relaxed your face and neck are.

Guided Imagery

Guided imagery is another way to meditate and relax. During this exercise, you'll sit or lie down and close your eyes. Then you will try to imagine what the speaker is saying. Don't think about anything other than what you're hearing. **Have the adult you're working with read the exercise on the next page while you're sitting or reclining in a comfortable place.**

Strategy 4

Guided Imagery Exercise

1. Close your eyes.

2. Imagine that you're at a playground with your friends. You wave to them and ask them to follow you to the swings. Once you get on a swing, you push your legs off the ground to get started. And then you swing back and forth, back and forth. You pump your legs to go higher and higher. You can feel the air blowing through your hair and on your face. You can see your friends smiling at you while they're swinging too. A friendly bee buzzes by your ear and then flies off to the field of flowers. As you slow down, you can smell the flowers and pine trees nearby. Then you and your friends jump off the swings, feeling the wood chips under your shoes as you land on the ground.

3. Now, slowly open your eyes and feel the calm.

Mindfulness

What does it mean to be mindful? *Mindfulness* means to pay attention to the present moment while being open-minded and accepting of yourself and your thoughts. Mindfulness can help you to pay better attention, have patience, and be in control of your thoughts and emotions. These are all skills that will be helpful when being kind to yourself and others. **Have the adult you're working with read the exercise on the next page aloud, and follow along.**

Strategy 4

The Mindful Walk Exercise

1. Turn off any electronic devices in the room.
2. Take a walk around the room.
3. Feel your feet and legs while you step on the ground. Notice your arms swinging.
4. Pay attention to your breathing while you're walking. Is it fast, slow, or medium?
5. What do you see when you're walking around the room? Is it cold, hot, or just right in the room?
6. Pay no attention to any thoughts in your head other than how your body feels and what you are experiencing in the moment.
7. If your mind wanders, refocus on your body.
8. If you're outside on your walk, what do you hear? What do you smell? What do you see? Is there a breeze, or is the air still?

You can learn to be mindful anytime! Just focus exactly on what's happening in that moment. When you're drawing, feel the crayon in your hand. When you're talking to a friend, focus on each word your friend says. When you're eating, feel and taste the food while it's in your mouth. Being mindful takes practice, and you can do it every day. Putting away your electronics for a short while can help too.

Strategy 5

Stay Calm

There will be times when you become upset and angry with others. During these times, it might be hard for you to be kind to them. But when you let your negative feelings buzz out of control, others' feelings will become intense too. Then you'll find that it's really hard for either of you to calm down and deal with the problem. But luckily, you've done a lot of great work in this book to learn about your emotions and how to relax! Because you have the skills, it's important for you to stay calm so you can be kind even when you're not happy. And remember, being calm doesn't mean you can't be upset and angry too. It just means you'll be able to think clearly. Staying calm during an argument can help the other person calm down, too, so you can fix the problem.

Remember to use your breathing exercises or mindfulness skills to relax so you can continue to be kind. Other ways to stay calm include taking a break in a quiet place, counting to 10, listening to music, or taking a walk. **Now, using the exercise on the next page, discuss how you can stay calm when dealing with a problem.**

Example from Buttercup

1. **What happened?**
   My friend yelled at me, saying that I didn't invite her to my birthday party. I forgot to stay calm and yelled back, saying, "I didn't want you there because you've been mean to me!"

2. **What I should have done instead?**
   I should have taken some deep breaths, and when I was calm, I should have said, "I'm really sorry. Being left out must have felt hurtful. I was upset because you were teasing me."

1. **What happened?**

2. **What I should have done instead?**

Now that you have learned how to be kind to yourself and express your emotions, let's learn how to be kind to others!

Strategy 6

Use Your Manners

Using manners means following rules of how you speak to and treat others. It's another way of being polite. You've probably learned manners from your parents, your grandparents, your teachers, and the other adults in your family. They might remind you to say "please" and "thank you" as a way of being polite. Being polite and using your manners is just one way of being kind to others.

See some examples of good manners on the next page.

How to Be Kind

Saying, "Excuse me," when you need attention

Saying nice things about how a person looks

Holding the door open for someone

Making good eye contact during conversations

Asking someone before using their things

Returning what you borrow

Knocking before opening a door

Saying, "I'm sorry," if you bump into someone

Picking your nose with a tissue

Using a napkin to wipe your face while eating

Saying, "Hello," to people

Giving an adult your seat if there are none left

Putting garbage in the trash can

Putting down your phone when with others

Not staring at others

Keeping your promises

Write a story or draw a picture about Buttercup the Bee using good manners.

Strategy 7

Slow Down and Pay Attention

Sometimes, we miss opportunities to be kind because we're rushing around and not paying attention to what's going on around us. While it's important to focus on your feelings, paying attention to how others are feeling is an important way to figure out what they might need to be happy. You can look at their facial expressions and body language, and you can listen to what they're saying to figure out how they might be feeling. **Complete the exercise on the next page to help give you clues about how to be kind to others.**

Field Trip Exercise

The next time you're at a store, in a restaurant, at the library, or at a park, stop and watch the people around you. Write down their behaviors, body language, and facial expressions and what you hear. How do you think they feel based on what you see and hear?

Strategy 8

Listen and Reflect

Another way to be kind to others is to be a good listener. When we have conversations, we're often thinking about what we're going to say next. This causes us to miss what the other person is saying. One way to show you're a good listener is to listen to what a person says and then *reflect*, or retell it in your own words. For example, if Buttercup the Bee says, "I was really upset the other day when Jenny told the teacher I was talking in class," you could say, "It sounds like you were really embarrassed and hurt that Jenny would do that to you because you thought she was your friend."

If you don't understand what they're saying or you didn't retell the information correctly, then you should ask more questions to help you understand. Open-ended questions are best because they give you more information. They are questions that don't have just a yes/no answer. For example, asking, "What did you do today?" is an open-ended question. Asking, "Did you have a good day?" only has a yes/no answer. A good listener should also make eye contact and use body language, such as nodding and smiling. Listening, reflecting, and asking questions help others know you really care about and understand them. **Now practice your skills with the exercise on the next page.**

Listen and Reflect Exercise

Reflect the statements from Buttercup the Bee below to retell what you think she's feeling and saying.

"My friend Gabe didn't want to play with me today."

"Jade said this hat looks silly on me."

"DeShawn got a better grade than me on the test."

"My pet ant died yesterday."

I forgot to study for the test and I'm worried I'll fail.
You're worried you will fail the test because you forgot to study.

Strategy 9

Compliment Others

Saying something nice about someone is another way to be kind. A compliment is a way to praise somebody or show that you admire them. You have to look for the good in people to give a compliment, which means that you care enough to spend the time to notice them. By giving somebody a compliment, you can help them feel good about themselves and improve their confidence.

You can give compliments to people in person, online, over the telephone, or by texting them. You can compliment someone's appearance, such as, "I really love your new haircut," but complimenting something they have done can have a bigger impact. For example, you could say, "The picture you drew in art class is amazing. You're a really talented artist." By complimenting somebody, you're also telling them to keep up the good work. You're rewarding and encouraging them to continue what they're doing. For example, the adult you're working with might say to you, "You're really putting in a lot of effort to learn to be kind. I'm proud of you, and you should be proud too." The more we notice and compliment others on their hard work, good deeds, and skills, the more likely these behaviors will continue. You're making the world a much better place by giving compliments. **On the next page, practice giving compliments.**

Giving Compliments to Buttercup the Bee

For the examples below, give compliments to Buttercup the Bee that focus on details. Be specific and honest.

1. **Buttercup just got a new haircut.**

2. **Buttercup flew in a race.**

3. **Buttercup stood up to a bully.**

4. **Buttercup set a new record in swimming.**

5. **Buttercup finished a painting in art class.**

I love
your new
glasses!
Thank you!

Strategy 10

Learn about Others

Being aware of differences and learning about them can help us be more loving and accepting of others. We may have different cultures, skin colors, abilities, communities, body shapes, experiences, religions, genders, and ages. We can live with different people, be from different places, and have different interests. By learning about others, we're telling them that they're important. We're also being respectful of their experiences and how those experiences have shaped them to be the people they are today. If you don't understand a difference, ask a trusted adult or read more about it. It shows kindness to celebrate diversity and the unique qualities each of us has. **In the following exercise, research a culture, religion, or race that is different from yours.**

What I've learned about: ____________________

Strategy 10

Now that you've learned a little about a culture, race, or religion, **interview a person who is different from you to learn more about them**. Just because a person is from a certain culture, race, or religion does not mean that they have all of the same interests or experiences, which is why it's also kind to learn about individuals. On the next page is a list of questions you can ask.

Interview

What do you like to do for fun?

What makes you proud?

Tell me about your family.

What is your favorite tradition?

What is your favorite food?

Tell me about your favorite holiday.

What do you like about your school or job?

What do you want people to know about you?

Strategy 11

Spend Time with Different People

Now that you've learned about some of the differences in others, it's important to spend more time with people who are different. In order to learn to be kind to a variety of people, we have to spend time with people other than just friends and family.

Getting to know people who are different from us, like those who come from different backgrounds, cultures, religions, and communities, can help us be open-minded and accepting, which is a way of being kind. And when we spend time with people who are different from us, any fear we might have fades away because we can see we are all just people who have different experiences. Spending time with people who are different from us can help us accept others and appreciate all of our differences.

Strategy 11

While we don't always have to agree with what other people believe, it's always important to be kind and accepting. This is called *tolerance*. Being tolerant means that you can spend time with people who are different from you and accept them for who they are. Tolerance can lead to the acceptance of others and allows you to learn about others' differences and experiences. The more we understand others, the easier it is to be kind. Also, the more we talk with people who are different from us, the more we find ways we are alike. We might find we are not as different as we once thought we were!

Field Trip Activity

With the adult you're working with, take a field trip to spend time with someone who is different from you. Write down or draw a picture of something new you learned about them.

Strategy 12

Volunteer

Volunteering means giving your time to causes in your community that need your help. Volunteering is a great way of being kind to others. You can volunteer to help people in need, animals, and the environment. By volunteering to help others, you're showing that they matter to you and you care. Helping others during their time of need is important if we want to build a kind community. **On the next page, think of ways you can volunteer and how those ways will help improve the lives of others.**

Example from Buttercup

1. **Buttercup wanted to volunteer to clean up the trash left around her neighborhood.**

   How will it help?
   By cleaning up the neighborhood, Buttercup will make the area beautiful and healthy.

Ways to Volunteer

1.

   How will it help?

2.

   How will it help?

3.

   How will it help?

Write or draw about a time that you volunteered, how you felt when you volunteered, and how volunteering changed your community for the better.

Strategy 13

Get Involved in My Community

In addition to volunteering, spending time in your community is a way to meet people and be kind. You can join a group with other kids, go to the park and meet new people, or cheer on your local sports teams. By getting involved in your community and with the people in it, you can build relationships and learn what your neighborhood needs in order to improve. You'll learn how to work with others in your community on a common goal to make the area a kinder place to live. **Now, use the skills you learned about paying attention and listening to figure out what your community might need and how you can help.**

Write down activities you can participate in or organize that will improve your community.

For example, Buttercup decided to sell her honey at a local stand and donate the money to her community food bank.

Strategy 14

"When They Go Low, I Go High"

In 2016, former first lady Michelle Obama said, "When they go low, we go high," as a way to handle and respond to bullies. Mrs. Obama meant that when people take the low road by being mean, it's important that we don't stoop to their level and also respond by being mean. When both people are bullies, no one wins, and the situation only becomes worse. Mrs. Obama added, "Going low is easy," but it doesn't solve anything, it doesn't make the world a better place, and it's definitely not the kind thing to do.

Taking the high road doesn't mean you can't be angry or stand up for yourself, but how you act toward others should be how you want them to act toward you. And as Mrs. Obama said, "You're response has to reflect a solution." That means that when someone is being a bully, your job is to help solve the problem and not make it worse. Sometimes "going high" means that you should ignore it when someone is being mean. Other times, it's an opportunity for you to try to figure out the real problem and solve it. "Going high" is another way to be kind to others, even when they're not being kind to you.

How would Buttercup "go high" in the following situations?

1. A kid in school says, "That shirt looks ugly on you, Buttercup."

2. A friend says something mean about Buttercup behind her back, and she hears it.

3. A girl pushes Buttercup down on the playground.

4. Buttercup asks to play a game at recess with the other kids, and they say no.

Strategy 15

Help Others

Although we already talked about volunteering, there are plenty of other ways we can help others. Helping others is a quick and easy way to be kind. Helping connects us to others while making our communities stronger and happier. You can do something simple, like picking up something that someone has dropped, or you can do something bigger, like raising money for a good cause. Even small kindnesses can brighten another's day.

Share a time when you were helpful.

Strategy 15

How can Buttercup be helpful in the following situations?

1. A person is holding a lot of packages and can't open the door.

2. A boy in Buttercup's class isn't doing well in math.

3. Buttercup has seen people in her city who are homeless and hungry.

4. A family member is stressed because there is so much to do around the house.

5. A girl in Buttercup's class forgot her lunch.

Strategy 16

Talk Before Posting

If you have social media accounts, you have an added responsibility to be kind when using these apps. Being kind on social media is not always easy or the common thing to do. Some people on social media find it easier to be a bully because they feel invisible or protected when they're not face-to-face with other people. Sometimes, people who aren't bullies in real life find themselves being bullies online because they feel stronger and bolder when they're invisible.

But bullying online can be just as harmful as bullying in real life. People who are bullied online often become sad and worried. If you think you're being bullied online, tell a trusted adult who can help you. In order to make sure you're being kind online and not bullying anyone, tell someone face-to-face what you're thinking about posting, or say it out loud to see if you think it's kind. Would you be offended by what you want to say? Would you be hurt if someone said it to you? These are important questions to ask yourself before posting on social media. And then, reread what you wrote before you post it.

Tell a story about Buttercup the Bee choosing not to post something that was offensive or mean after she reread it and why she made that choice.

Strategy 17

Put Myself in Another Person's Shoes

Putting yourself in another person's shoes means imagining what a person might be feeling and having compassion for them. This is called *empathy*. By having empathy, you have a real interest in other people's lives, and you believe that what they go through, feel, or experience is important. Having this understanding is another way to show kindness. Empathy also includes trying to understand how your actions affect others.

In order to understand how others might be feeling or what they might be thinking, it's important to first use the listening skills you practiced earlier in this book. Then, you need to pay attention to their emotions through their body language and facial expressions. What are they trying to communicate? Finally, it's important to show that you value a person's feelings and experiences by acknowledging them. For example, when you see that Buttercup isn't sharing her toys, you could say, "I know it's really hard to share because you want to play with those toys too." **On the next page, what do you think Buttercup might be thinking and feeling? How would you feel if you were Buttercup?**

Strategy 17

What is Buttercup thinking and feeling?

1. Buttercup has a new baby brother.

2. Buttercup is moving to a new state.

3. Buttercup was teased for needing a wheelchair.

4. Buttercup's skin color is different from everyone else's in her class.

5. Buttercup found out she was adopted.

Using empathy, watch a television show or movie. Pause the show throughout and discuss how the characters might be feeling and what they might be thinking. Write about what you've learned.

Name of the television show or movie: ______________________

Strategy 18

Stand Up for Others

Standing up for others is another way to be kind. It means that you speak for those who don't have a voice, like babies or animals. You can also stand up for people when you feel like they're being taken advantage of or not being treated respectfully. Sometimes people can't or don't stand up for themselves because they're afraid or nervous. By standing up for others, you're letting them know that they're important to you. It's also a way to build trust and show that you're loyal. Standing up for others takes courage and strength. It's important to be kind by being a defender of justice and a protector of those who cannot protect themselves.

Make up a story about Buttercup, who has the superpower of standing up to others.

Strategy 18

How should Buttercup stand up for these people?

1. Buttercup sees her friend being teased because she got a bad grade on her test.

2. Buttercup's classmate is being left out of the soccer game at recess.

3. Buttercup's friend is being made fun of because of his skin color.

4. No one will sit next to a girl at lunch.

You're too small to play with us. Go away!
Please be nice. They can play with us.

Strategy 19

Share

People have probably been teaching you to share since you were really young. Sharing is such an important skill because you'll have to share throughout your life. While it can be hard to share some of your favorite things, keep in mind how good you feel when others share their things with you. Sharing helps you learn how to compromise and be fair to others. Plus, sharing is another easy way to be kind and show others you care about them. You know you can share your toys and possessions, but you can also share your time, skills, love, and knowledge. **On the next page, write down some of the things you can share with others.**

What are some things you can share?

With an adult, work together to color this picture. You'll have to compromise on the colors you use and share coloring materials.

Strategy 20

Be Forgiving and Ask for Forgiveness

No one is perfect, and everyone makes mistakes, including adults and children. That's why it's important to forgive others for making mistakes. Forgiving others gives them the chance to change, learn, and improve. You're giving them another chance to be a better person by being kind, even when they've made a mistake or done something wrong. And hopefully you'll get the same opportunities to improve when you make mistakes.

Being forgiving doesn't mean that you've forgotten what has happened or feel that the actions are right. Forgiveness means letting go of any thoughts of getting revenge or any anger you have toward people because of something they've done wrong. It takes a strong person to be forgiving. When you forgive someone, you can say how the actions made you feel and then let the person know that you hope he or she can act differently next time.

How should Buttercup be forgiving in the following situations?

1. Buttercup's friend lost her sweatshirt that he borrowed.

2. A girl in school was mean to Buttercup's friend at recess.

3. After he had a bad day at work, an adult yelled at Buttercup.

It's important for us to take responsibility for our actions if we've been unkind or made a mistake. Admitting that we've made a mistake or done something wrong can be really scary and embarrassing. Many people don't have the strength to be so responsible. But you've learned a lot, and admitting to your mistakes and poor behavior will help you learn how to behave differently next time. You're confident, and confident people own up to their mistakes. That's what's so important about mistakes—they help us learn and grow. After we take responsibility, we have to ask others for forgiveness. By admitting that we've done something wrong and then asking for forgiveness, we are being kind to others and showing them that we care about how our behavior affects them.

Share a time when you made a mistake and asked for forgiveness. What was it like? How did you feel?

How Being Kind Has Affected Me

How do you feel when you're kind to others? What benefits do you get when you're kind?

My Own Be Kind Strategies

Write down other Be Kind strategies you developed.

1.

2.

3.

The End of This Book Is Just the Beginning of Being Kind

You've learned a lot of ways to be kind to yourself and others, and you've come up with some of your own strategies to be kind while reading this book. Through these exercises, you learned that people can be different but still have important experiences you can learn from and appreciate. You've learned the importance of standing up for others and how making mistakes is just an opportunity to grow. But most importantly, you've learned that while being kind may take practice, it's easy to do and makes you and others feel happy and accepted.

How to Be Kind

People will not always be kind to you, but that says more about who they are than who you are. Remember, when someone is unkind, they're probably hurting in some way. They might lack confidence, be afraid, or have trouble understanding how their actions affect others. But you're a great role model. You can be kind and show that you're still a strong person by standing up for yourself and others. You'll notice that being kind helps others hear what you're saying more than arguing and being hurtful. And your kindness will rub off on others.

Remember, there are many more kind people in the world than unkind people. Finding good people is easy to do ... you just have to keep your eyes open to see all the beauty the world has to offer. And you're a big part of that beauty. Just like a bee takes pollen and spreads it around the world so all of the amazing plants and flowers can grow and blossom, you can spread beauty by being kind. Just like there is no end to the plants and flowers, there is no end to the kindness you can give to yourself and others. So, take what you've learned and spread your goodness.

Acknowledgments

First, thank you to Karen South, Susan Thompson, Jennifer Gilpin-Yacio, John Yacio, and the team at Future Horizons for taking a chance on a first-time author and championing this book. Your guidance and support have been immeasurable. Thank you to my colleagues and the staff at Laughlin Children's Center, who are so passionate about the work we do and were so encouraging when they heard about the book. In particular, thank you to Sharon Campbell, who jumped in to promote this book with vigor and excitement. Thank you to Giuseppe F. for your gracious help in digitizing my artwork and ensuring the integrity and vibrancy was maintained. I have so much appreciation for Val W. and Michelle W. for being just as excited as I am about this endeavor and for all of your amazing ideas for promoting this book! Thank you both! Mandie G. and Dana G.—you two were the first to read the book, and you edited and provided notes with enthusiasm, even when you did not know if this project would leave my computer. For your hard work, collaboration, and unwavering support, I am extremely grateful. Moreover, Mandie, thank you for being the best sister. Your encouragement and sense of humor are very much appreciated. I do not have any comparisons, but I know you are the best of the best. You are also raising such kind humans, and I find that inspiring! Thank you to my parents Toni and Jake Z. who show up daily, without fail, to support anything I decide to undertake. You both are my constant cheerleaders and the best role models on how to navigate this world with thoughtfulness and compassion. I really won the parent lottery with the two of you. Silvio and Milena, you both inspire my desire to see this world become a kinder place and seeing how you act with empathy and kindness is exceptionally encouraging. Thank you to numerous family members and friends, including but not nearly limited to Amy C., Jen C., Andrew G., Andy G., Louann N., Linda R., Mark R., Tiffanie S., Jim W., Kathy W., Ryan W., and Alex W., for your constant love and support. I am so lucky to have such strong and thoughtful people in my life like all of you. Finally, Jim, thank you for supporting me throughout this journey and for always looking out for my best interests. You were so patient when our dining room became an art studio, and you have encouraged me to believe in myself and my work. My appreciation and love for you is beyond words.

Written & Illustrated by
Kristie Zoller, PsyD

817.277.0727 | fhautism.com

www.ingramcontent.com/pod-product-compliance
Lightning Source LLC
Jackson TN
JSHW040229280825
90087JS00001BA/1